ROSÉ MADE ME DO IT

ROSÉ MADE ME DO IT

60 PERFECTLY PINK PUNCHES AND COCKTAILS

COLLEEN GRAHAM

ILLUSTRATED BY RUBY TAYLOR

Andrews McMeel
PUBLISHING®

Andrews McMeel Publishing
a division of Andrews McMeel Universal
1130 Walnut Street, Kansas City, Missouri 64106

www.andrewsmcmeel.com

20 21 22 23 24 HPL 10 9 8 7 6 5 4 3 2 1

ISBN: 978-1-5248-5992-3

Library of Congress Control Number: 2019957469

ATTENTION: SCHOOLS AND BUSINESSES

Andrews McMeel books are available at quantity discounts with
bulk purchase for educational, business, or sales promotional use.
For information, please e-mail the Andrews McMeel Publishing
Special Sales Department:
specialsales@amuniversal.com.

MIX
Paper from
responsible sources
FSC™ C007454

This book is produced from independently certified FSC™ paper
to ensure responsible forest management.

For more information visit: www.harpercollins.co.uk/green

CONTENTS

INTRODUCTION

Rosé isn't a wine that fits conveniently into one category in terms of style, grape, or flavor profile—it's a complex group that includes sweet, dry, still, and sparkling wines produced all over the world!

There are, however, three things that rosés do have in common: they're pink (although they vary from pale to surprisingly dark), they pair well with food, and they're fabulous cocktail mixers, the latter being the focus of this book. I won't boggle your mind with the ins and outs of rosé (although you will learn a bit about how it's made and what to expect from certain regions or grape varietals)—there are plenty of books out there that cover all of the finer details. Instead, I want to invite you on a journey of discovering rosé cocktails! Rosé is one of the best wines for mixed drinks, with its flavor of strawberries or watermelon. It works perfectly with many spirits (whiskey, gin, vodka, tequila, rum) and almost any additional flavors, from fruits to herbs and spices. And although seen as a summer wine, it's a great fit for cocktails at any time of year.

My goal is to give you some basics on mixing up great cocktails, and to inspire you to explore some unusual flavors. This book includes some incredibly simple drinks—like the Pink Wine Spritzer (see page 32)—as well as a rosé twist on familiar drinks like the mojito and the gin and tonic. There are some very special cocktails that display unique flavor combinations, such as the Lychee Ginger Martini (see page 107) and the Rosemary & Basil Fizz (see page 119). And you'll find that I love to use homemade ingredients. Of course, given the topic, there are also plenty of frosé and sangria recipes. I've found inspiration in the drinks that others have created, and hope to inspire you to take these to a new level. I'm not a wine critic or expert, but a writer who has spent over a decade studying mixed drinks and is grateful to be able to share that knowledge with others. Cocktails are meant to be fun, and wine should be fun. When the two come together, you know a party's on its way!

WHAT IS ROSÉ?

In nature, there are red grapes and white grapes, and within those, hundreds of varietals are used to make red and white wine respectively. There are, however, no pink grapes, so how does one get the pink wines designated as rosés?

Rosé is not defined by the grape, but by the method. The catch is that since rosés are not varietal-dependent like other styles of wine, they offer a vast range of flavor profiles. There are sweet rosés, a surprising number of dry rosés, and plenty of sparkling rosés to choose from. Rosés are made in every corner of the globe, although there are areas in major wine-making countries that specialize in it. You will notice regional differences at times, just like with other wines, and you will encounter bottles that are a complete gamble. Will it be sweet or dry? Sometimes it's very hard to tell, but that's part of the fun!

If your experience with rosé has been limited to white zinfandel (yes, the sweet wine that captures the attention of many young drinkers is a rosé), then you'll be delighted to know that there really is a rosé for every wine drinker.

HOW IS ROSÉ MADE?
There are a few different methods for making rosé. The most common one that is used today begins with the juice of red grapes remaining in contact with the grape skin for a few days before the skin is removed. This short period of maceration results in a blush-colored wine.

A few rosés use a direct pressing method whereby the grapes are pressed with the skins, which are then removed straight away, leaving behind a light pink juice.

A third approach is the *saignée* process (pronounced sehn-yay, French for "to bleed"). In this case, a little of the red wine juice is "bled off" early in the maceration process while the wine is still pink. The result is both a usable rosé and a red wine.

Used less often, a fourth technique involves blending a red and white wine together. Some wine-making regions frown upon the method, and many don't regulate it, but a number of rosé Champagnes rely on it.

STYLES OF ROSÉ

Rosé is French for "pink"; Spanish and Portuguese wines are labeled "rosado," and Italian wines "rosato." However, rosé is definitely not limited to these countries. Understanding the complex maze that is rosé's many flavor characteristics is complicated, so we'll only touch on this briefly to make navigating wine labels a little easier.

Rosé comes in many shades of pink. On the lightest side, you'll find the drier rosés of Provence. This French region primarily makes rosé, offering zesty, refreshing wines that have long been held up as the standard. Following these are the pinot noir rosés, which are slightly earthier, with a bright, acidic fruitiness. Spain's favorite grape—the tempranillo—produces a slightly darker rosé with a brilliant spiced-berry flavor and a slightly darker hue. Surprisingly, when it comes to the rosé color spectrum, California's famed white zinfandel falls right in the middle. If you're looking for a sweet wine, a bottle of white zin is what you want.

As you move through the remaining red wine grapes, the rosés produced by them tend to get darker. From merlot and sangiovese to cabernet sauvignon and shiraz (or syrah), the pink begins to resemble red wine. The darkest rosés come from Tavel, a small area in France's Rhône Valley that produces nothing but rosé. These offer the best choice for red wine lovers, with the perfect display of tannins against spicy berry flavors and an unusually dry palate.

All of the other styles of rosé produced throughout the world fall somewhere within that spectrum. There are great options from Germany (roséwein or Weissherbst), France's Loire Valley (rosé d'Anjou), and the Austrian state of Styria. The Spanish rosados (including sparkling cavas) are light and fresh, while Portugal tends to produce rosados that are sweet and inexpensive, with a hint of sparkle. Moscato wines are sweeter, and Italy's prosecco rosatos are known for their vivacious bubbles. Beyond all that, there are many rosés that don't fit into any easily defined idea of regional or varietal characteristics.

Before we finish, there are just a few more simple notes to bear in mind. The driest rosés often come from the driest red wine grapes, such as grenache, cinsault, and shiraz. Any rosé can be a blend of grapes or use a single varietal, so don't rely on that. A sparkling wine with a label saying "frizzante" is gently sparkling, and "brut" means "dry." When in doubt, simply read the winemaker's notes on the label. And, if you're intrigued by a bottle (even just the catchy label), try it! If you don't like it on its own, there's bound to be a cocktail that will doctor it up.

DRINKING ROSÉ

Despite all the variations, rosé always has a generalized flavor profile of strawberries or watermelon. It contains fewer tannins than red wines and is very easy to drink. Rosés are typically best when young, too, so drink them up, don't store them!

For the most part, you'll want to chill still rosé before drinking it, and sparkling rosés are best when ice cold. You are free to stick to your own preferences, but since we're mixing up cold rosé cocktails here, keeping bottles cold will definitely help the drinks along.

You will also be delighted to hear that rosé is the most versatile wine for food pairings. Don't stress over which wine is best with steak or seafood—rosé can cover the entire gamut of foods, cuisines, and courses, from canapés to dessert. Likewise, the cocktails you make with rosé will be a splendid match for any meal.

TIPS FOR PERFECT COCKTAILS

Here's the secret to mixing up a great cocktail: have fun!
There are lots of tricks that bartenders use to create spectacular drinks, but anyone can learn the basic techniques (they're not difficult), so the most important thing is to have a good time. You might make mistakes—we all do—and that's okay. It's just a drink that will be gone in a few minutes; the real joy in mixing cocktails is the exploration, discovering what you like and don't like.

That said, a few tips will help you make the best cocktails possible:

• Use premium-quality spirits that you wouldn't mind drinking on their own. There's no need to pay for a super-pricey bottle of rosé, though, as wine is typically a cocktail mixer that allows you to save a bit of money.

• Fresh ingredients are best. This is particularly true of citrus juices, but if you have the ability to juice other fruits, say with an electric juicer, that's even better. And don't be afraid of homemade mixers like Simple Syrup (see page 15)—they're easy, cheap, and fun.

• Chill your glassware, especially if the cocktail recipe doesn't include ice in the glass. Your drinks will stay colder longer and be more refreshing.

If you find a drink that you think needs to be tweaked, by all means do it! Cocktail recipes are meant to be adjusted according to personal taste, and everyone's tastes are different. After all, I'm not drinking it—you are.

BAR GEAR

There's no need to buy a full bar kit unless you'd like to. With just a few of the essentials, you can mix up a great variety of drinks.

A cocktail shaker is a must. A standard three-piece shaker with a built-in strainer will do most home bartenders just fine. Stainless-steel shakers are the best and will last a lifetime. If you go the pro route and pick up a Boston shaker (one piece is a shaking tin and the other a mixing glass), be sure to buy a Hawthorne strainer as well.

A bar spoon is also a good investment because the long, twisted handle makes stirring a breeze, especially in tall glasses. For precise measuring, a jigger (a double-sided cup that measures shots and half-shots) is invaluable and allows for the greatest control of flavor balance. Add a fine-mesh strainer for straining. Finally, add a muddler to your shopping list. The freshest cocktails—mojitos and juleps included—require this handy stick, resembling a miniature baseball bat. (More on this on page 12.)

ICE

It's a given that high-quality ingredients will produce better-tasting mixed drinks, and the same rule applies to ice. It is the one ingredient that almost every cocktail has in common, so it's extremely important!

You will use a lot of ice, both in the serving glass and/or the cocktail shaker. Make your ice with distilled water for the best results, and do always have a fresh stock of ice in the freezer so that you don't run out. If there's a tray that's been sitting there for a couple of months unused, toss it away and start again. Try to avoid storing ice near fish and other pungent frozen foods, too, because it will absorb some of their flavors. Fishy drinks are definitely not good!

For a drink like the Berry Rosé Julep (see page 31), you'll need shaved ice (okay, it's not necessary, but it is really nice). If you don't have an ice maker that has that capability, toss some ice in your blender and give it a few whirls, then get rid of any excess water. Another fun way to crush ice (a little chunkier than shaved ice) is to whack it with your muddler. Put some ice cubes in a sealable plastic bag or a Lewis bag (made of cloth just for this purpose) and whack it into smaller bits. It's also an activity that provides great stress relief!

A couple of the recipes also utilize novelty ice cubes as part of the drink. The Rosé Parade (see page 92) freezes wine into ice cubes, while the Sparkling Borage Cocktail (see page 71) and the Blushing Fizz (see page 96) both freeze flowers inside the ice.

SHAKING AND STIRRING

There are two primary methods for mixing cocktails: shaking and stirring. They're both easy, but there are tricks to doing it right. For the first, fill the cocktail shaker with ice (about five or six cubes). Shake for at least 10 seconds or until the outside of the shaker gets nice and frosty. Some drinks are stirred and you'll want to do this with a smooth, steady turn of the wrist (keep your elbow still, it's not cake batter!) for at least 30 seconds.

With either technique, always strain out the mixing ice unless the recipe indicates otherwise. The agitation during mixing breaks down the ice so it will melt faster, resulting in a drink that quickly becomes watered down. For drinks served on the rocks, use fresh ice in the serving glass.

MUDDLING

The fresher the drinks you want to mix up, the more you will fall in love with muddling. It's a fantastic mixing technique used to juice the majority of fruits and to extract the essence from herbs, creating a flavorsome crushed base for a drink out of fresh ingredients. Once you learn the value of a muddler, you'll wonder where this amazing tool has been all your life!

12

The process of muddling is incredibly simple: place the ingredients to be muddled in the bottom of a mixing glass or shaker and press them with the flat end of the muddler until well mixed (a minute or two usually does it). Use a twisting motion with your wrist as you push down to accentuate the mixing.

Fruits that are to be muddled should be cut into small pieces (an inch or so). Citrus fruits work well as half slices and wedges, and there is no need to remove the peel. For leafy herbs like mint and basil, tear the leaves or slap them between your palms before dropping them into the glass to maximize the flavor. Other herbs (such as lavender and rosemary) and spices can be tossed in whole, as long as any stems have been removed beforehand.

SPARKLING ROSÉ
Quite a few of the recipes you'll find in this book call for sparkling rosé. If you already have a bottle of still rosé open, don't rush to the shops for a bottle of bubbly; you can mimic sparkling rosé by adding a little soda water to still rosé. Just a couple of splashes in a glass or so of wine will give a nice effervescence without overly diluting it. The other option is to add a splash of soda water directly to the drink after pouring the still wine.

SANGRIAS AND PUNCHES
We're dealing with wine recipes here, so you should expect to find a few sangrias and other wine punches. Each recipe was written for 6 fluid ounce servings, and the number of servings each recipe produces is indicated. If you need more or less punch, simply increase or decrease each ingredient accordingly, as long as you always keep the ingredients in proportion.

You'll also see that the sangria recipes suggest "marrying" the flavors by chilling the drink overnight. This is the best way to create punches that use fresh fruits. As they sit, the liquids absorb the taste of the fruits, giving you a concoction the following day that is one beautiful blend of flavors!

IN THE BLENDER

Yes, even rosé can end up in a frozen cocktail! If you haven't enjoyed a frosé yet, you're in for a real treat. For the best blended drinks, chop the ice and any fruits in the blender before adding the liquid ingredients.

Most recipes call for around a cup of ice, which is five or six average-sized cubes. After blending, if the result is a little too thin for your taste, add one or two more ice cubes and blend again. And if the cocktail is too thick? Add a splash of one of the drink's liquid ingredients.

DRESS IT UP

Garnishes are often an afterthought, especially if you're just mixing up a drink for yourself. But they do look pretty, and they can help to make a good impression when serving guests, so it's a good idea to practice creating them as often as you can. Additions such as citrus slices and twists, as well as herbs, can add to the flavor of a drink, too. You can squeeze a little juice in as you drink, gently press a lemon twist over the cocktail to express its essence, or drop in something like rosemary and let the herb's flavor slowly infuse into the liquid. The smallest touches often take a cocktail from okay to spectacular.

Rimming a glass is another fun option that can be used with almost any cocktail. In these pages, for example, you'll find the No Way Rosé Margarita (see page 55), which calls for a sugar rim. Begin by wetting the rim of the glass with a liquid in the recipe (with many cocktails, a citrus wedge works perfectly). Then roll the rim of the glass around in a small dish filled with white granulated sugar until it's coated evenly. Still holding the glass upside down, gently tap off any excess sugar and you're ready to pour the drink. This fancy little trick goes a step further with the Birthday Cake Mimosa (see page 95), in which you'll dip the rim first into some delicious frosting, followed by some colored sprinkles!

SYRUPS

As much as I love to muddle, my fascination with Simple Syrup is even greater. It is the one ingredient in the bar that you have absolute control over, and it's the perfect sweetener for cold drinks because the sugar's already been dissolved before it is added to the drink.

Many of the recipes in this book rely on homemade syrups with bespoke flavor infusions that you'll be hard pressed to find in stores. All of these are made using Simple Syrup, and details of these are given on page 17. And plain Simple Syrup itself is used even more often; once you learn its dirty little secret, you'll never waste your money buying it again!

What is Simple Syrup? Water and sugar! It's really that simple. In a pinch, you can even combine the two ingredients in your cocktail shaker, shake it up, and *voilà*. That's called "bar syrup," and it will do, but there is a standard Simple Syrup recipe that you'll turn to time and again on your cocktail adventures:

In a small saucepan, bring 8½ fluid ounces of water to a boil. Add a heaped cup of sugar and stir constantly until it has dissolved completely. Cover the pan, reduce the heat, and then simmer for 15 minutes. Let the syrup cool before bottling it in a tightly sealed jar. This will produce 8½ fluid ounces of syrup, which will keep well in the refrigerator for a week or two.

Now that you know the secrets to Simple Syrup, it's time to add flavor! The possibilities are endless, and you can make single-ingredient syrups or create custom blends with complementary flavors. These homemade syrups provide a great way to get the taste of fresh ingredients into an easy-to-mix sweetener.

The additional ingredients you'll need to add to the basic syrup recipe in order to create each of the homemade syrups mentioned in this book are provided opposite. The individual recipes will then guide you through the process of making them.

> For all syrups, the general technique is to add the flavoring ingredient (chopped fruit or whole herbs and spices) after turning the syrup down to a simmer, then taking the pan off the heat and letting it steep in the syrup until it has cooled down completely. Before bottling, strain out any solid pieces so that you are left with a clean-flavored syrup.

Use the syrup for the intended cocktail, then explore its potential in other drinks—any syrup can be topped with soda water for a homemade soft drink, many will work as a sweetener for lemonade or iced tea, and some are perfect for hot drinks like coffee and tea (especially the cinnamon syrup).

Three recipes call for honey syrup, which enables you to add the flavor of honey to a drink in a form that is easier to mix. Honey syrup is made with equal parts of honey and water, stirred until they reach a uniform consistency. You can make just enough for each cocktail.

FLAVORED SYRUPS USED IN THE RECIPES

Lavender Syrup: used in the Lavender Pink Lemonade (page 43); add 3 tablespoons of lavender flowers.

Rose Syrup: used in the No Way Rosé Margarita (page 55); add 4 fluid ounces of rose water.

Strawberry Syrup: in The Frosé (page 56); add 3 large strawberries and ¼ teaspoon of vanilla extract (optional, but recommended).

Basil Syrup: used in the Watermelon Frosé (page 64); add 1 cup of basil leaves.

Borage Syrup: used in the Sparkling Borage Cocktail (page 71); add a handful of borage flowers and young leaves.

Rosemary Syrup: used in the Rosaquiri (page 76); add 1 or 2 sprigs of rosemary.

Thyme Syrup: used in the Rosé Sour (page 79); add 5 large sprigs of thyme.

Vanilla-Lavender Syrup: used in the Blushing Fizz (page 96); add ¼ ounce of lavender buds and 1 vanilla pod.

Sage-Lime Syrup: used in the Sage Gimlet (page 100); add a few sage leaves and the juice of 1 lime.

Lychee Syrup: used in the Lychee Ginger Martini (page 107); add scant ½ cup of hulled fresh lychees.

Rosemary-Basil Syrup: used in the Rosemary & Basil Fizz (page 119); add 1 sprig of rosemary and 1 cup of basil leaves.

Cinnamon Syrup: used in the Poinsettia Sangria (page 123); add 1 cinnamon stick.

Plain Honey Syrup: is found in the Sweet Honey Rosé (page 104) and the Rosé Collins (page 115) recipes. The Tea for You & Me recipe (page 84) adds the juice of a lime to honey syrup.

INFUSIONS

Another fun way to add a twist of flavor to cocktails is with the use of infusions. Infusions are created using a spirit—most often vodka or rum, although other spirits are not off-limits. Some of the flavors you'll find in the recipes can be found commercially, but others will not be available, so you will need to create these at home.

Homemade infusions are even easier to make than flavored syrups, though most take far longer. You'll need to plan ahead—anywhere from a day to several weeks—to allow the flavors to develop fully; when that is will be a matter of personal taste, but guidelines are given in each case. The only tools you'll require are infusion jars (wide-mouthed with a tight seal and large enough to hold the desired amount of alcohol), a straining system (a fine-mesh strainer and/or some muslin), and a knife to cut up any ingredients. Beyond that, all you'll need is patience.

Fruits need to be rinsed and cut up; spices can be left whole, and entire sprigs of herbs can be used once rinsed. Place the ingredient in a jar, fill it with the alcohol, shake, then leave it in a cool, dark place. Shake the jar once a day to wake everything up. Taste the infusion toward the end of the time and let it rest longer if needed. Once the flavor reaches your desired intensity, strain out the solid ingredients and bottle your new spirit—no refrigeration is needed.

Generally, the quantity of flavoring ingredient is not dependent on the amount of alcohol—two tea bags will infuse a bottle of rum just as well as they will flavor 3 fluid ounces of rum for a single drink. The volume difference may simply require a longer or shorter infusion time. However, it is worth making at least half a bottle at a time, since you can then use the infusion in other cocktails. The homemade infusions that you'll need for some of the recipes in this book are shown opposite. As with the syrups, full instructions are then provided within the relevant recipes.

INFUSIONS USED IN THE RECIPES

Chili-infused Citrus Vodka: used in the Spicy Spritzer (page 36); starting with a citrus vodka (buy it or make your own), you'll need 2 whole chilis and an infusion of just 2 hours (it gets hot very fast).

Citrus-infused Vodka: (extremely easy to find commercially): potentially used for the chili-infused citrus vodka above, but needs to be done separately and first because citrus fruits require a much longer infusion. Use a combination of lemons, limes, and oranges (1 of each fruit for an entire bottle works well) to create a custom blend. Rinse the fruit and cut into slices. Infuse for 3 days to a full week.

Pomegranate-infused Vodka: (very easy to find commercially): used in the Pomegranate Grapefruit Frosé (page 63); requires the arils (seeds) of 1 pomegranate crushed in vodka, and infused for 5 days.

Tea-infused Rum: used in the Tea for You & Me (page 84); requires 2 tea bags and a 1-day infusion.

Grapefruit-infused Tequila: used in the Rosé Sunrise (page 103); requires 1 whole grapefruit, cut into slices, and an infusion of 3 to 5 days.

Ginger-infused Vodka: (very limited commercial availability): used in the Lychee Ginger Martini (page 107); requires 1 cup of sliced ginger and about 7 days for the infusion.

Cucumber-infused Vodka: (limited commercial availability): used in the Rosemary & Basil Fizz (page 119); requires 1 cucumber and potentially 2 weeks of infusing.

Mango-infused Rum: (commercially available): used in the White Peach Sangria (page 127); requires 1 mango and at least a week for the infusion.

THE RECIPES

ROSÉ 75

(Makes 1)

One of the best-known Champagne cocktails around, the French 75 has been a favorite celebratory drink since it was created sometime around World War I. As you can imagine, it has taken a number of turns over the last century. In fact, it's rare to find two identical French 75 recipes. So let's keep changing it up, skip the Champagne, and pour a sparkling rosé instead! Rosé is a lovely wine for this simple drink, and the pink bubbles give it a new life in the glass. While the majority of drinkers today prefer gin in a French 75, brandy (specifically Cognac) has been an option for years and it's actually a slightly better fit for rosé. This is especially true if you have a drier wine—the brandy will add a delectable hint of sweetness that gin simply can't provide.

Ingredients
1 ½ fluid ounces brandy
¼ fluid ounce Simple Syrup (see page 15)
½ fluid ounce fresh lemon juice
sparkling rosé, to top off
a lemon twist, to garnish

Instructions
In a cocktail shaker filled with ice, combine the brandy, Simple Syrup, and juice. Shake well and strain into a flute. Top off with sparkling rosé and decorate with a lemon twist.

ROSÉ & TONIC

(Makes 1)

The Rosé & Tonic is a little dry and a little sweet, which makes
it a fabulous dinner drink. Pair it with seafood, or any meat
or vegetarian dish that features plenty of savory herbs and
spices, and you're in for a real treat. Tonic water has a dry
profile and is a natural palate cleanser, so it's always an
excellent companion to a meal. Rosé is also a very versatile
wine for food pairings, and it contributes a touch of
sweetness. The lime brings it all together, adding a hint
of tartness both in the drink and on your lips. It's a delightful
balance that can make almost any meal more enjoyable.

Ingredients
3 fluid ounces rosé
3 fluid ounces tonic water
a lime wedge

Instructions
Pour the wine into a tall glass filled with ice, then add the tonic
water. Rub the lime wedge around the rim of the glass, then
squeeze the juice into the drink and drop in the wedge.

ROSÉ MOJITO

(Makes 6-8)

Mojitos are a ton of fun to drink and not as hard to make as you might think. The secret is to use a muddler to press the fresh mint into the syrup. This flavor foundation can then be dressed up in the original way (rum and soda water) or it can take a more unconventional turn, as with the Rosé Mojito. "Refreshing" doesn't even begin to describe the taste; you'll love how the cooling, sweetened mint plays off a nice rosé. It is then given an extra twist by using a sparkling lemonade rather than soda water. If you prefer it less sweet, add a lemon-flavored Italian soda water instead.

Ingredients

2 limes, cut into wedges
1 cup fresh mint leaves
Simple Syrup (see page 15), to taste
25 fluid ounces rosé
16 fluid ounces sparkling lemonade
lime slices and extra mint leaves, to garnish

Instructions

Using a muddler, press the lime wedges, mint leaves, and about ½ fluid ounce of Simple Syrup in a jug to release the juice and essential oils. Add the rosé and lemonade. Stir well, taste, and add more syrup if desired. The jug can then be stored in the refrigerator for an hour or two. Serve in tall glasses filled with ice and garnish with lime slices and fresh mint.

Tip: If your mint is beginning to wilt, you can make a mint-infused Simple Syrup ahead of time instead (see page 16). Use a lot of mint so that the flavor is intense—you then won't have to add more syrup later, which would result in an overly sweet drink.

STRAWBERRY MOJITO

(Makes 1)

Strawberry season is the perfect time to mix up this delightful mojito for yourself. Sweet, juicy strawberries go perfectly with rum and mint and take the place of the cocktail's traditional limes—and of course there's a rosé twist that you're going to love. You'll find this cocktail to be an excellent place to use your favorite light rum—most will pair perfectly with any rosé you choose. Although you will muddle the strawberries, mint, and syrup, it's not a bad idea to use an old bartender's trick to wake up the mint—simply slap the leaves in the palm of your hand before adding them to the glass. It's a quick step that can have quite an impact on the drink's flavor.

Ingredients
3 strawberries, hulled and sliced
a handful of fresh mint
½ fluid ounce Simple Syrup (see page 15)
1 ½ fluid ounces light rum
3 fluid ounces rosé
soda water, to top off
an extra strawberry and a sprig of mint to garnish

Instructions
In the bottom of a tall glass, muddle the strawberries, mint, and Simple Syrup. Fill the glass with ice and add the rum and wine. Stir well, then top off with a splash of soda water. Garnishing the drink with a single strawberry and a small sprig of mint is a nice finishing touch.

BERRY ROSÉ JULEP

(Makes 1)

The Berry Rosé Julep puts a berrylicious twist on the classic mint julep. It's perfect for warm weather affairs, whether you're enjoying some time with friends or just want to slip out onto the patio for a relaxing afternoon in the sun on your own. Choose a nice, smooth whiskey for this drink—something like a softer bourbon or an Irish blended whiskey is ideal against the fresh berries. This drink also substitutes rosemary for the traditional mint, creating a sweet floral touch that is quite lovely against the pink wine. Add more berries if you like, and mix raspberries with blackberries if you have both on hand.

Ingredients
5–6 raspberries and/or blackberries
a sprig of rosemary
1½ fluid ounces whiskey
rosé, to top off
extra rosemary and berries, to garnish

Instructions
In the bottom of a tumbler, muddle the berries and rosemary. Add the whiskey, then fill the glass with shaved ice. Top off with rosé, garnish with rosemary and a few berries, and enjoy it through a paper straw.

PINK WINE SPRITZER

(Makes 1)

Sometimes you will open a bottle of rosé only to find that it's
not quite what you expected. That doesn't necessarily mean
it's bad—it may simply need a little help. In these moments,
turn to the Pink Wine Spritzer, a simple recipe that can give
any rosé a boost. There are no fancy tricks here, just a little
sparkling soda water added to a still rosé. The key is to make
sure that both ingredients are well chilled before mixing
them. Not only is this a great drink on its own, and fabulously
easy to mix up, you will also find it useful if you want to
create a cocktail that calls for sparkling rosé, but you don't
happen to have a bottle of the bubbly version available.
In fact, soda water added to any still wine will allow you
to enjoy the same sparkling effect for very little cost.

Ingredients

3 fluid ounces chilled rosé
1 fluid ounce ice-cold soda water

Instructions

Pour the rosé into a white wine glass, then top it off with the
ice-cold soda water.

ROSÉ APEROL SPRITZ

(Makes 1)

The Rosé Aperol Spritz is a great drink to accompany a meal. It pairs well with a variety of foods, from seafood to red meat, and is fabulous with multi-course dinners that involve a wide variety of flavors. It's a refreshing and easy cocktail worthy of any dinner party. Aperol is an orange-colored aperitif with a bitter orange flavor that will wake up your taste buds and get them ready for the delicious food that you've prepared. While this drink is often made with a sparkling white wine, it's extra special when prepared with a sparkling rosé. The soda water is there to give the bubbles a boost.

Ingredients
2 fluid ounces Aperol
3 fluid ounces sparkling rosé
a splash of soda water
an orange slice, to garnish

Instructions
Fill a white wine glass with ice, then add the Aperol and sparkling rosé. Top with a splash of soda water and decorate the glass with the orange slice.

SPICY SPRITZER

(Makes 1)

Rosé is not out of the question when you're in the mood for a spicy cocktail. You simply have to treat the two flavors in a delicate manner and keep things simple. That's exactly what you'll find in the Spicy Spritzer, a funky twist on the Pink Wine Spritzer (see page 32). The spice in this cocktail comes from a quick infusion of chili in a citrus vodka. You can use any type of chili, although Thai chilis and jalapeños are excellent choices. Then, to balance the drink, use soda water if you have a sweeter rosé, or ginger ale if the wine is on the drier side.

Ingredients
2 chilis
1½ fluid ounces Chili-infused Citrus Vodka (see page 19)
3 fluid ounces rosé
a splash of soda water or ginger ale
an orange slice, to garnish

Instructions
Make the chili-infused vodka as hot as you like. This is a fast infusion, so keep testing it and remove the chilis as soon as it reaches your desired intensity—the longer you leave the chili in, the spicier it will get. Pour the infused vodka and wine into a tumbler filled with ice. Top with a splash of soda water or ginger ale, stir, and add an orange slice.

GLAMOUR GIRL MARTINI

(Makes 1)

Mix up the girliest of all pink martinis and enjoy a very fruity cocktail. This is definitely one to make for special occasions, and it's a fabulous choice for bachelorette parties, birthday parties, and anniversaries. With the Glamour Girl Martini, you'll enjoy the fruity combination of peach and cranberry backed by pink wine. It's a lovely drink and, as an added bonus, the wine base makes it lighter on the alcohol than most regular martinis, so one drink won't leave you tipsy.

Ingredients
3 fluid ounces rosé
1 fluid ounce peach schnapps
½ fluid ounce cranberry juice
a maraschino cherry, to garnish

Instructions
Pour all three ingredients into a cocktail shaker filled with ice. Shake well, strain into a chilled martini glass, and top with a cherry.

ROSÉ COSMO

(Makes 1)

The classic cosmopolitan is an ideal cocktail for a little rosé. It already has the sweet fruits that pair so nicely with rosé, and the recipe is not too different from the original, so it's both familiar and novel. For the Rosé Cosmo, the wine and citrus vodka play equal roles to form a pretty foundation. This then gets a slight accent from triple sec and cranberry juice to produce a well-balanced cocktail that's easy to drink. In true cosmopolitan fashion, add as much cranberry juice as you like; this recipe produces a drier cosmo that can easily be sweetened by doubling or tripling the juice.

Ingredients
1½ fluid ounces Citrus-infused Vodka (see page 19)
1½ fluid ounces rosé
½ fluid ounce triple sec
½ fluid ounce cranberry juice
an orange twist, to garnish

Instructions
Combine the ingredients in a cocktail shaker filled with ice and shake well. Strain into a chilled martini glass and decorate the rim with an orange twist.

LAVENDER PINK LEMONADE

(Makes 1)

On a hot summer day, nothing is quite as refreshing as a tall glass of lemonade. It's incredibly easy to make lemonade from scratch—all you need is sugar, lemon juice, and water. A glass of Lavender Pink Lemonade gives that formula a funky, fresh twist. This recipe begins with a lavender-infused syrup and is best made with freshly squeezed lemon juice. The water of traditional lemonade is then replaced with a good dose of rosé, which turns this popular drink into a stunning wine cocktail for an afternoon in the garden. Though the recipe makes just a single glass, it's easy to mix up for a party. Simply keep the syrup and juice equal at one part each, then use three parts wine. Pour it all into a jug with ice and stir well. Be sure to sample it and adjust the sweet and sour ingredients to suit your taste.

Ingredients
1 fluid ounce Lavender Syrup (see page 17)
1 fluid ounce fresh lemon juice
3 fluid ounces rosé
a lemon wedge, to garnish

Instructions
Pour the Lavender Syrup, lemon juice, and rosé into a cocktail shaker filled with ice and shake well. Strain the drink into a highball glass filled with fresh ice and complete it with a lemon wedge.

WATERMELON CUCUMBER COOLER

(Makes 1)

Watermelon and cucumber go together like strawberries and cream. This garden-fresh duo is used to make some amazing cocktails, and the Watermelon Cucumber Cooler is one of them. The gin you choose to pour into this drink will make a big difference. While juniper-forward options like a traditional London dry gin make a good drink, it's even better with a gin that has a softer profile. Two favorites are Hendrick's and Aviation American Gin; the former features rose petals and cucumber, while the latter has a floral bouquet dominated by lavender. There are other gins that would work wonderfully, too—just keep in mind that you want to accent (not contradict) the sweet and cooling fruits.

Ingredients
2 cucumber slices
3 watermelon cubes
½ fluid ounce Simple Syrup (see page 15)
1½ fluid ounces gin
½ fluid ounce lime juice
3 fluid ounces sparkling rosé
an extra cucumber slice and a watermelon wedge, to garnish

Instructions
In the bottom of a tall glass, muddle the cucumber, watermelon, and Simple Syrup thoroughly to release all the fruit juices. Fill the glass with ice, then add the gin, lime juice, and sparkling wine, and stir well. Decorate the glass with the extra cucumber and watermelon.

KIR

(Makes 1)

A staple of French cafés, the Kir has been a popular wine cocktail for decades because of its fabulous simplicity. It was popularized by Félix Kir, the mayor of Dijon in Burgundy after World War II, who frequently served this local drink to show off two of the area's finest products—wine and crème de cassis. It remains an impressive cocktail today, and deserving of the French treatment. When it comes to creating a balanced drink, the Kir is best with a dry wine because the blackcurrant liqueur is very sweet. The rosés produced in France's Provence region are absolutely perfect because they tend to be among the driest pink wines produced. While the regular Kir is made with still wine, you can also make a Kir Royale with a sparkling rosé, or a Kir Imperial with a still rosé and Chambord. No matter how you make it, this one's a great choice for dinner.

Ingredients

½ fluid ounce crème de cassis
chilled dry rosé, to top off
raspberries, to garnish

Instructions

Pour the crème de cassis into a stemmed wine glass, then top off with rosé. Garnish with a few raspberries floating in the drink.

ROSÉ BELLINI

(Makes 1)

A popular choice for brunch, the Bellini is a fabulously simple cocktail. It offers a delightful peach background for sparkling wine and will pair wonderfully with all of your favorite mid-morning foods. In the Rosé Bellini, the customary Champagne is replaced with a sparkling rosé. The drier your wine, the better—the peach nectar imparts enough sweetness to balance out the drink. And this recipe doesn't just swap in the rosé; it is also made a little bit rosier with a splash of rose water, which adds a lovely floral touch—just make sure it's food-grade. While it's highly recommended and accents this peach cocktail perfectly, it can be skipped and you can still enjoy a delightful drink.

Ingredients
2 fluid ounces peach nectar, juice, or purée
sparkling rosé, to top off
a splash of rose water

Instructions
Pour the peach nectar into a flute. Top off with sparkling rosé, then add a splash of rose water.

PINEAPPLE MIMOSA

(Makes 1)

Mimosas for everyone! This sparkling orange cocktail is an absolute joy to play around with, as there are so many fruity possibilities to try. One popular rendition is the Pineapple Mimosa, which gives the drink a tropical spin that's perfect for a summertime brunch. This recipe produces a drink that is just a little stronger than the average mimosa because it uses pineapple vodka. The pineapple doesn't stop there, either! To double up on the flavor, you blend pineapple juice with orange juice before adding your chosen sparkling rosé. Have fun with the garnish, too. With the help of a cocktail stick you can make an elaborate "flag" using a pineapple wedge and a cherry to really dress up the glass.

Ingredients

1 fluid ounce pineapple vodka
½ fluid ounce triple sec
½ fluid ounce orange juice
½ fluid ounce pineapple juice
sparkling rosé, to top off
a pineapple wedge and a cherry, to garnish

Instructions

Pour the vodka, triple sec, and both juices into a flute. Top off with sparkling rosé and garnish with a pineapple–cherry skewer.

POMEGRANATE MIMOSA

(Makes 1)

As festive as it is lovely, the Pomegranate Mimosa will allow you to carry your love for mimosas into the winter. It's the ideal cocktail for a holiday brunch, when you can pick up a fresh pomegranate and harvest the arils (seeds) for a seasonal garnish. The pomegranate flavoring, though, comes from pomegranate liqueur. This is typically ruby red and creates a stunning-looking cocktail. You can also make a fresh grenadine (pomegranate-flavored syrup) to use instead, and even mix that with a little vodka to create your own rendition of the liqueur. The soda water is added to boost a still rosé, but you can pour a sparkling rosé and skip the soda water if you prefer. If you're feeling particularly merry, a sprig of rosemary makes a fun garnish. This will infuse slowly in the drink and create a subtle but sensational extra layer of flavor.

Ingredients

1 ½ fluid ounces pomegranate liqueur
½ fluid ounce triple sec
3 fluid ounces rosé
a splash of soda water
pomegranate arils (seeds) or rosemary, to garnish

Instructions

Pour the liqueur and triple sec into a flute and add the rosé. Finish the drink with a splash of soda water for sparkle, and decorate the glass with a few pomegranate arils or rosemary.

NO WAY ROSÉ MARGARITA

(Makes 1)

If it seems like you can add rosé to nearly any cocktail, that's because you can! The classic margarita is definitely not off-limits, and it's a lot of fun when you add the flavors of both rosé and rose. The No Way Rosé Margarita is based on the original margarita recipe, which is fantastically refreshing and easier to mix up than most people think. In this variation, we keep the margarita's traditional trio of tequila, lime juice, and triple sec, then add a rose-flavored syrup and a little rosé. It's a simple twist but a lovely one, and an absolute delight to drink.

Ingredients
a splash of Rose Syrup (see page 17)
white sugar
1 ½ fluid ounces tequila
1 fluid ounce fresh lime juice
½ fluid ounce triple sec
2 fluid ounces rosé
a lime twist, to garnish

Instructions
If desired, moisten the rim of a cocktail or margarita glass and dip it in sugar. In a cocktail shaker filled with ice, combine all the ingredients. Shake well, then strain into the prepared glass and garnish with a lime twist.

THE FROSÉ

(Makes 6)

It may have started as a trend, but The Frosé is a drink that will be enjoyed for many years to come. And if there is one cocktail that rosé is specifically known for, this is it! It has been instrumental in the pink wine's rise in popularity over the last few years. The Frosé is, essentially, a slushie in which you can blend any variety of fruits. The basic recipe features strawberries, which is the best fruit pairing for rosé. You can add the fruit to some Simple Syrup to make a strawberry-flavored syrup (see page 17 for quantities), but it's much easier to toss it directly into the blender. And a supply of washed, hulled, and sliced strawberries (or any fruit of choice) kept in the freezer will make things even quicker. With any frosé, the wine will lose a bit of color and flavor, so it's best to choose a darker, fuller-flavored rosé.

Ingredients
2 cups strawberries, hulled and sliced
1 cup ice
25 fluid ounces rosé
2 tablespoons white granulated sugar, or to taste
extra strawberry slices, to garnish

Instructions
Put the strawberries and ice in a blender and blitz lightly. Add the rosé and sugar, then blend until smooth. Pour into tall, chilled glasses and garnish with strawberry slices. If it's not thick enough, add a little more ice—you may need as much as 2 cups, depending on your preference—and blend again. Likewise, add more sugar if you'd like it sweeter. You can also store any excess frosé in the freezer until you're ready for another drink.

COCONUT & MANGO FROSÉ

(Makes 1)

Cool down on a hot summer day with a delicious Coconut & Mango Frosé. It's sweet and inviting, with a tropical flavor that is sure to transport you to some faraway island paradise. The recipe comes with a couple of options for two of the ingredients; choose whichever you prefer or is easiest to find. While coconut rum is very common, if you can find a coconut-flavored vodka, you might enjoy that a little more. Likewise, if you can't find fresh mangoes at the grocery store, pick up some mango nectar instead.

Ingredients

2 fresh mango slices or 1 fluid ounce mango nectar
1 cup ice
1 fluid ounce coconut rum or vodka
3 fluid ounces rosé
½ fluid ounce lemon juice
½ fluid ounce Simple Syrup (see page 15)
mango and lemon slices, to garnish

Instructions

Place the mango and ice in a blender and blitz lightly. Add the other ingredients and blend until smooth. Pour into a stemmed tall glass and garnish with slices of mango and lemon.

BLACK FROSÉ

(Makes 1)

Sometimes you just have to step away from the cute pink drinks and mix one up that's dark and mysterious. While there are no secrets to the Black Frosé, it does have a deep purple color that is a complete change of pace from most rosé recipes, which is what makes it so much fun. This is probably one of the easiest frosé variants you can make because it requires just four simple ingredients. The fruits are then backed up by a shot of Chambord, although you can substitute any other black raspberry liqueur you like.

Ingredients
⅔ cup blackberries
1 cup ice
1½ fluid ounces Chambord
3 fluid ounces rosé
extra berries, to garnish

Instructions
Place the berries and ice in a blender and give them a quick blitz. Add the Chambord and wine, then blend until smooth. Pour into a tall hurricane glass, or piña colada glass, and garnish with a few berries.

CHAMBORD

BLACK RASPBERRY LIQUEUR
PRODUCT OF FRANCE
70cl   16.5% Vol

POMEGRANATE GRAPEFRUIT FROSÉ

(Makes 1)

A beautiful blushing pink, the Pomegranate Grapefruit Frosé is as stunning to look at as it is to drink. This wine slushie deserves some beautiful glassware, so pull out a piece of your fancy stemware to serve it in—a coupe, a large red wine glass, or a margarita glass. The flavor combination of pomegranate and grapefruit is an absolute delight. Pomegranate vodkas are easy to find, but you can also make your own using the fresh fruit when it's in season. It just so happens that the pomegranate and grapefruit seasons coincide in the middle of winter, so this frosé is a wonderful way to forget about the cold for a few minutes!

Ingredients

1 cup ice

1 fluid ounce Pomegranate-infused Vodka (see page 19)

3 fluid ounces rosé

1 fluid ounce grapefruit juice

a splash of lemon juice

½ fluid ounce Simple Syrup (see page 15)

a sprig of fresh mint or thyme, to garnish

Instructions

Blitz the ice in a blender, then add all of the ingredients and blend until smooth. Pour into a large coupe or red wine glass and garnish with a sprig of mint or thyme.

If you choose to make the pomegranate-infused vodka, add the arils (seeds) to a clear vodka in an infusion jar. Crush the arils using a muddler to release their juice, then let it sit for about 5 days before straining and bottling.

WATERMELON FROSÉ

(Makes 6)

The beauty of frosés is that you can use all sorts of ingredients to create them. Quite often, you can take inspiration from flavor pairings used in foods, such as fruit salads. That's what happened with this Watermelon Frosé, and it is certainly not a one-dimensional taste! It turns out that both watermelon and blueberries are a perfect match for basil, and all three are really nice against a rosé background. While the herb itself does not blend well, a simple syrup that extracts the flavor from its leaves does. The Watermelon Frosé is perfect for a summer barbecue, so it's made by the jug. After all, something this delicious is too good to keep to yourself.

Ingredients
2 fluid ounces Basil Syrup (see page 17)
1 cup watermelon, cubed
1 cup blueberries
1 cup ice
25 fluid ounces rosé
2 tablespoons sugar, to taste
watermelon wedges, blueberries and basil leaves, to garnish

Instructions
Place the watermelon, berries, and ice in a blender and blitz lightly. Add the Basil Syrup and the other ingredients and blend until smooth (adding more ice if you prefer a thicker drink). Pour into tall glasses (Mason jars are ideal) and garnish each with a small watermelon wedge, a few blueberries, and a basil leaf.

SOMETHING BLUE

(Makes 1)

When you're tired of mixing all the pink cocktails, switch to Something Blue (literally!). This beautiful and elegant cocktail was designed for weddings and bachelorette parties, but is a perfect fit for any special occasion—or just an afternoon with friends. The star of this show is Hpnotiq, an alluring ocean-blue liqueur that's filled with tropical fruit juices, French vodka, and a kiss of Cognac. The taste really does live up to the description, and it is spectacular with a dry rosé. Although this recipe makes a single glass, this is another one that can easily be made by the jug. Keep the quantities of liqueur and wine equal, then add half as much ginger ale just prior to serving to ensure it's delightfully bubbly.

Ingredients
2 fluid ounces Hpnotiq
2 fluid ounces dry rosé
a splash of lemon juice
1 fluid ounce ginger ale
a lemon twist, to garnish

Instructions
Pour the liqueur, wine, and lemon juice into a flute. Top with the ginger ale, then garnish with a long lemon twist draped over the rim.

PIMM'S & ROSÉ

(Makes 1)

A British favorite, Pimm's No. 1 Cup is typically served with sparkling lemonade and enjoyed while watching tennis! The Pimm's & Rosé puts a twist on that classic drink, giving it a lovely kiss of blush wine while maintaining the traditional sparkle. This tall drink is very easy to mix up, and just as easily increased to fill a jug. The garnishes are key to the experience, so if you normally skip dressing up your drink, don't do that here. The cucumber adds a great hint of flavor, and borage is an herb with a similar taste (use the flowers, leaves, or both). You can also add any combination of orange slices, strawberries, or mint. Each garnish will contribute to the drink's flavor, so have fun customizing it with any produce you find appealing as you shop.

Ingredients
1 fluid ounce Pimm's No. 1 Cup
3 fluid ounces sparkling rosé
3 cucumber slices
borage or mint leaves, to garnish
strawberries and orange slices, to garnish

Instructions
Pour the Pimm's into a tall glass filled with ice. Top with the sparkling wine, then add cucumber slices, some borage or mint, berries, and orange slices.

SPARKLING BORAGE COCKTAIL

(Makes 1)

Borage is not found in many cocktails, but it can be used to make some amazing drinks. The herb's flowers and young leaves taste surprisingly like cucumber. It takes on a dual role in the Sparkling Borage Cocktail, a floral martini that's sure to enhance your summer afternoons. For this recipe, you will need to make two ingredients with borage ahead of time—some borage ice cubes and a borage-flavored syrup. If you don't grow your own borage, make sure you source it from somewhere that doesn't spray the plants with chemicals. Avoid older leaves as they lose their flavor; if you get pricked by a leaf, it's too old so don't use it.

Ingredients
a handful of borage flowers and young leaves
½ fluid ounce Borage Syrup (see page 17)
1 ½ fluid ounces gin
½ fluid ounce elderflower liqueur
a splash of lime juice
sparkling rosé, to top off

Instructions
Choose a few flowers that are in pristine condition to freeze into ice cubes: fill the tray halfway with distilled water and freeze, then add a flower to each cube, fill with water, then freeze again. It should take just over a day. When you are ready to serve, add a few borage ice cubes to a chilled cocktail glass. Shake the Borage Syrup, gin, liqueur, and lime juice with ice, then strain into the glass. Top off with sparkling wine.

ROSY RASPBERRY PRESS

(Makes 1)

A fresh take on the popular vodka press, this is a tall, refreshing, and very fruity cocktail. It's a lot of fun to mix up and will give you a chance to learn a new bartending skill if you're up for the challenge. The vodka press is a rendition of the Presbyterian, a whiskey highball that pairs soda water and lemon–lime soda. This recipe puts yet another twist (or three) on the recipe: muddling fresh raspberries and lime slices, switching to raspberry vodka, and skipping the second soda in lieu of sparkling rosé. The common way to mix a press is by "rolling." It's a technique bartenders like to use to show off, whereby you "roll" a drink by pouring it back and forth between two glasses. Make sure your glasses are about the same size—pint glasses and cocktail shakers work well—and that they aren't filled to the rim. You might want to practice with iced water first. If you don't want to risk a spillage, just go ahead and stir the drink instead.

Ingredients
5 or 6 raspberries
2 lime slices
2 fluid ounces raspberry vodka
2 fluid ounces sparkling rosé
2 fluid ounces soda water

Instructions
In the bottom of a highball glass, muddle the raspberries and lime slices. Fill the glass partially with ice, add the vodka, wine, and soda water, then roll the drink (or stir). If needed, add a couple more ice cubes before serving.

COCONUT

WATER

AGUA DE
COCO

LIGHT PIÑA COLADA
(Makes 1)

Typically made with rum and cream of coconut, the piña colada is a perennial summertime cocktail. Why not try switching to a sweeter rosé wine and coconut water for a lighter version that is even more refreshing but has all the wonderful flavors you've come to love? The key to a really well-made piña colada is to give the drink a good shake before serving. The pineapple will froth up and, when it's strained, create a luscious foamy top that invites you in for each sip.

Ingredients
2 fluid ounces rosé
1 ½ fluid ounces coconut water
1 fluid ounce pineapple juice
a splash of lime juice
a pineapple wedge or lime slice, to garnish

Instructions
Pour the ingredients into a cocktail shaker filled with ice. Shake well then strain into a chilled coupe glass, garnishing with a pineapple wedge or lime slice.

ROSAQUIRI

(Makes 1)

Freshly made daiquiris beat any mix you can buy from a shop, and the recipe is so simple that it's a shame not to mix one up from scratch. The basic recipe requires rum, lime juice, and Simple Syrup, with no secret ingredients. But as you would expect, we're going to add a spin to that recipe to create the fabulous Rosaquiri! Beyond adding rosé wine to the mix, this recipe uses a rosemary-flavored syrup. It adds a lovely floral note to the cocktail, and you can use any leftover syrup to jazz up a simple glass of lemonade, or to sweeten a wine spritzer (see page 32).

Ingredients
½ fluid ounce Rosemary Syrup (see page 17)
2 fluid ounces rosé
1½ fluid ounces aged rum
½ fluid ounce lime juice
an extra sprig of rosemary and a lime wheel, to garnish

Instructions
Pour the Rosemary Syrup and all of the other ingredients into a cocktail shaker filled with ice and shake well. Strain into a chilled coupe glass and garnish with a small sprig of rosemary and a lime wheel.

ROSÉ SOUR

(Makes 1)

The Rosé Sour transforms the classic whiskey sour into a beautiful drink to enjoy on a sunny day. It begins with a yellow Chartreuse rinse, which leaves your glass kissed with herbal sweetness. A smooth Irish whiskey and sweet rosé form the base, while the sour citrus is offset by a thyme-infused syrup. Egg white tops it all off with a luscious foam. Some people are reluctant to drink raw egg—and you can still enjoy this drink without it—but it's perfectly safe, as long as your egg is as fresh as possible. If you have concerns, try a quick freshness test: place the egg in a glass of water and if it sinks to the bottom, it's good!

Ingredients
1 teaspoon yellow Chartreuse
white of 1 egg
½ fluid ounce Thyme Syrup (see page 17)
1 ½ fluid ounces Irish whiskey
1 fluid ounce sweet rosé
1 fluid ounce lemon juice
2 dashes of orange bitters
lemon zest, to garnish

Instructions
Rinse a cocktail glass with yellow Chartreuse by pouring in the liqueur, rolling it around to coat the inside of the glass, then getting rid of any excess. In a cocktail shaker without ice, dry-shake the egg white for about 10 seconds to break it up. Add ice and all the other ingredients. Shake vigorously for about 30 seconds, then strain into the prepared glass and garnish with a touch of lemon zest.

ROSÉ ROYALE

(Makes 1)

Pisco is a style of brandy produced in Peru and Chile, which is famously used to make a pisco sour. That delicious recipe is transformed here into the equally tasty Rosé Royale, where it gets a kiss of sweet elderflower from a touch of St-Germain liqueur. In true pisco sour fashion, an egg white is added to lend a tempting foam. As with the Rosé Sour (see page 78), the egg is perfectly fine to drink raw, as long as it is very fresh. The base of the Rosé Royale is an enchanting mix of pisco, elderflower, lime, and rosé. The addition of bitters on top then gives it an elegant touch that delights you at first sip.

Ingredients
white of 1 egg
1½ fluid ounces pisco
½ fluid ounce St-Germain liqueur
½ fluid ounce lime juice
2 fluid ounces rosé
3 dashes of Angostura bitters

Instructions
Place the egg white in a cocktail shaker and dry-shake it for about 10 seconds. Fill the shaker with ice, then add the pisco, liqueur, lime juice, and rosé. Shake vigorously for 30 seconds and strain into a coupe glass. Finish with 3 dashes of bitters in the foam.

GREEN & PINK LEMONADE

(Makes 1)

Green lemonade is great fun to make, and it's a recipe that is completely adaptable. It can be made with tequila, vodka, and whiskey, or alternatively it can be booze-free. It's also a perfect fit for rosé wines of any style. In the Green & Pink Lemonade, a sparkling rosé is a great choice, although you can achieve the same effect by pouring a still wine and adding a spritz of soda water. Fresh kiwis and equal parts limeade and lemonade are the common denominators in all of my green lemonade renditions. Kiwis are perfect against the sweetened citrus juices, and they're absolutely adorable as a garnish. Another lovely aspect of this recipe is that you can mix up the base and have a jug ready in the fridge, just waiting to be topped off with your choice of bubbly.

Ingredients
4 kiwi slices, skin removed
¾ fluid ounce Simple Syrup (see page 15)
1 ½ fluid ounces limeade
1 ½ fluid ounces lemonade
3 fluid ounces sparkling rosé
1 extra kiwi slice, to garnish

Instructions
Muddle the kiwi slices and Simple Syrup in the bottom of a tall glass. Fill with ice, then add the limeade and lemonade, finishing with the sparkling wine. Garnish with a slice of kiwi.

TEA FOR YOU & ME

(Makes 2)

Afternoon tea for two can be made more interesting when you bring rum and rosé into the mix. This recipe is simple but unique, using a tea-infused rum as its base. White rum works best, but you can use any tea you like—green or black, or blends such as Earl Grey. Adding rosé and a lime–honey syrup, topped off with the drier profile of tonic, creates a well-balanced drink to enjoy with a friend.

Ingredients

8 fluid ounces water
4 fluid ounces honey
juice of 1 lime
3 fluid ounces Tea-infused Rum (see page 19)
4 fluid ounces rosé
2 fluid ounces tonic water
4 dashes of celery bitters (or orange bitters)
lime wedges, to garnish

Instructions

Bring the water to a boil in a small saucepan, then add the honey and lime juice. Stir, cover, reduce the heat, and simmer for 5 minutes. Remove from the heat and leave, covered, to cool. It can be stored in a sealed container in the refrigerator for up to a week. For the cocktail, fill two tall glasses with ice. Pour the ingredients in order, starting with the tea-infused rum and the honey syrup, equally between the two glasses. Stir well and garnish with the lime wedges.

CELERY BITTERS

1864

honey

THREE
HILLS

RESERVE ROSÈ
FRUITY & DRY

2019

SUMMER ROMANCE

(Makes 1)

Creamy and fruity, you're sure to fall in love with the
Summer Romance. This sweet tequila blend makes a
delightful after-dinner drink on a relaxed summer evening.
Tequila is classified according to how long it is left to age.
Reposado tequila is a lightly aged style that spends around
two to nine months in oak barrels, giving the agave-based
spirit a pleasant oak flavor that works wonderfully when
mixed into a cocktail. Here it is blended with the spiced
honey taste of Benedictine liqueur and sweet raspberries.
The coconut lends a luscious creaminess, while the sparkling
rosé ensures a lively finish.

Ingredients
6 raspberries
1 ½ fluid ounces reposado tequila
½ fluid ounce Benedictine
½ fluid ounce cream of coconut
2 fluid ounces sparkling rosé
extra raspberries, to garnish

Instructions
Muddle the raspberries in the bottom of an old-fashioned
glass. Add ice, then pour the remaining ingredients in order.
Stir well and garnish with a few extra raspberries.

LA ROSA PALOMA

(Makes 1)

Rosé and strawberries are a fun way to dress up the popular tequila-based cocktail, the paloma. As with the original recipe, this appealing variation features the refreshing taste of grapefruit, which comes into play via a flavored sparkling water, making it a great choice for summer, and particularly enjoyable for an afternoon picnic. La Rosa Paloma is a quick drink to mix up, too. While you might be tempted to skip the rosemary garnish, give it a try if you have the herb around. A small sprig will slowly infuse its flavor into your drink as it sits on top, providing a graceful finishing touch. You can also add a little rosemary into the muddle for a stronger taste.

Ingredients

½ fluid ounce lime juice
2 strawberries, sliced
1 ½ fluid ounces blanco tequila
2 fluid ounces rosé
3 fluid ounces grapefruit-flavored sparkling water
1 grapefruit slice and a sprig of rosemary, to garnish

Instructions

In the bottom of a highball glass, muddle the lime juice and sliced strawberries. Fill the glass with ice, add the tequila and wine, then top it off with the sparkling water. Finish with a grapefruit slice and rosemary sprig, to garnish.

PINK NEGRONI

(Makes 1)

The Negroni is a fabulous aperitif that can be enjoyed before any meal. The original gin-and-Campari recipe has been remade many times since its creation in the 1920s. One of the most popular variations gives it a bubbly twist, and in the Pink Negroni, we're going with a lovely French rosé Champagne. Campari is the key to any negroni. This Italian aperitif has a bitter flavor that takes some getting used to, but it pairs perfectly with gin, and this recipe offers a particularly gentle introduction to the Campari taste, softening it with port (tawny or ruby ports are best) and the sweet black raspberry addition of Chambord. It's an elegant cocktail worthy of a special dinner, no matter what's on the menu.

Ingredients
1 fluid ounce gin
½ fluid ounce Campari
½ fluid ounce port
¼ fluid ounce Chambord
rosé Champagne, to top off

Instructions
Pour the gin, Campari, port, and Chambord into a flute. Top off with rosé Champagne and let the bubbles do the mixing for you.

ROSÉ PARADE

(Makes 1)

The Rosé Parade is definitely a fun rosé martini—the emphasis here is on the presentation, which makes the tropical fruit flavor even more enjoyable. The fun begins with rosé ice cubes, which are then adorned with three balls of fresh papaya. The drink itself is a combination of guava nectar and sparkling rosé, and there's no mixing involved—the bubbles take care of that for you. The rosé cubes mean that you can enjoy this one as slowly as you like, too; you won't need to worry about ending up with a watered-down drink, no matter how warm the weather is.

Ingredients
5 rosé ice cubes (see below for added flair)
3 papaya balls
1 fluid ounce guava nectar
3 fluid ounces sparkling rosé

Instructions
Make the rosé ice cubes by filling an ice cube tray with still rosé wine. Add fruits or herbs such as raspberries or rosemary to the cubes if you like. Let them freeze overnight and remove them from the freezer just before making the cocktail. Use a melon baller to scoop out balls of papaya. (These can also be frozen ahead of time, if you prefer—simply spread them out in a single layer to keep them separate.) Place 5 rosé cubes and 3 papaya balls in a cocktail glass. Top with the guava nectar and finish with the sparkling rosé.

BIRTHDAY CAKE MIMOSA

(Makes 1)

This adorable-looking mimosa is the ultimate way to celebrate someone's birthday! The drink is pretty delicious, too, recreating the yummy flavors of a sweet birthday cake in a flute. The base of this cocktail is a mix of sweet cake-flavored vodka (whipped-cream vodka also works well) and coconut water. A sparkling rosé then gives it the mimosa touch. But it's the rim of this cocktail, with its vanilla frosting and colorful sprinkles, that truly transforms it into a drink to toast someone's special day.

Ingredients
vanilla frosting (buttercream)
colored sprinkles
1 ½ fluid ounces cake-flavored vodka
½ fluid ounce coconut water
sparkling rosé, to top off

Instructions
Dip the rim of a flute into a dish of vanilla frosting, rolling it around to get a good coating. Then dip the rim into a second small dish filled with colored sprinkles. Pour the cake-flavored vodka and coconut water into the prepared glass, then top off with your sparkling rosé.

BLUSHING FIZZ

(Makes 1)

The Blushing Fizz features vanilla-lavender syrup, an ingredient that's a personal favorite and useful for creating the loveliest drinks. Here, that soft flavor is paired with the spicy sweetness of ginger liqueur (Domaine de Canton is an excellent choice). Sparkling rosé then invigorates the blend to create a highly enjoyable drink. This recipe also features another fun ingredient—lavender ice cubes, which can be made by adding lavender flowers to a filled ice cube tray before freezing. You can also make the cubes a little sweeter by adding some of the vanilla-lavender syrup.

Ingredients
1 fluid ounce Vanilla-Lavender Syrup (see page 17)
½ fluid ounce lemon juice
1½ fluid ounces ginger liqueur
lavender ice cubes
sparkling rosé, to top off
a lemon twist or edible flowers, to garnish

Instructions
In a cocktail shaker filled with ice, combine the syrup, lemon juice, and liqueur. Shake well then strain into a tall glass filled with lavender ice cubes. Top off with rosé then garnish with a lemon twist; or if you're in the mood to get fancy, decorate this cocktail with edible flowers—roses, nasturtiums, borage, and hibiscus are all fun options. Just ensure that the plants have not been sprayed with pesticides or other chemicals—even if you're not going to eat the garnish (a social faux pas, but who's looking!).

ROSÉ POPTAIL

(Makes 1)

Poptails are the adult answer to frozen popsicles, and you can add all sorts of alcohol, juice, and fruits. The Rosé Poptail is a great introduction and, because wine is the only alcohol involved, you'll have no problems getting it to freeze. Popsicle molds are easy to find and usually make four to six ice pops at a time. Because the sizes vary, this recipe is written in parts rather than exact measurements. Simply figure out the total volume needed and divide it between the two liquids. (Or make a little more than you need and enjoy any leftovers while you wait for the popsicles to freeze!) Don't forget to buy the sticks if your mold doesn't include them.

Ingredients
½ part ruby red grapefruit juice
1 part rosé
raspberries
blackberries

Instructions
Combine the grapefruit juice and wine in a jug and stir well. Fill each mold three-quarters of the way up. Add a few berries to each mold; when you do this will depend on where you want them placed. For berries at the top of the popsicle, add them right away because they will sink in the mold. If you want berries in the middle and closer to the stick, add them after the mixture has become slushy. You can also add a berry or two later in the freezing process for even distribution. Once all the berries are in place, top off the molds with your wine-juice mix. A fun way to serve these is to chill a Mason jar, then fill it halfway with a chilled sparkling wine. Turn a Rosé Poptail upside down and stick it in the glass. You get an iced wine to drink and an edible treat at the same time!

SAGE GIMLET

(Makes 1)

Simple, sophisticated, and offering a lovely mix of flavors, the Sage Gimlet puts a wine-and-herb twist on a cocktail that has long been a favorite. Typically, a gimlet is nothing more than gin and lime cordial, and this recipe keeps it fairly simple. The key ingredient here is the sage–lime syrup; adding this to a full-flavored gin, then finishing it off with a soft rosé, creates a cocktail that is perfect for an afternoon in the garden.

Ingredients
½ fluid ounce Sage–Lime Syrup (see page 17)
1½ fluid ounces rosé
1½ fluid ounces gin
an extra sage leaf, to garnish

Instructions
In a cocktail shaker filled with ice, combine all the ingredients then shake well. Strain into a chilled cocktail glass and garnish with a single sage leaf floating on top.

HECHO EN MEXICO

Marnier-Lapostolle

CORDON ROUGE

Dulce Vida
GRAPEFRUIT

100% PURE AGAVE   HANDCRAFTED
70 PROOF

GRAPEFRUIT REAL GRAP

Maison Fondée en 1827

Grand Marnier
LIQUEUR
ORANGE & COGNAC

PARIS-FRANCE

ROSÉ SUNRISE

(Makes 1)

The tequila sunrise is a showy cocktail filled with fruit flavors, which has led to its immense popularity over the years. It's also the perfect recipe for a twist, and the Rosé Sunrise definitely throws in a few. This drink allows Grand Marnier to take over the orange element, while a grapefruit-infused tequila enhances the citrus aspect. Instead of orange juice, it's filled with brut (dry) rosé, giving it a lovely balance and softer profile. The grenadine not only produces the signature sunrise effect, but also adds a sweet pomegranate fruitiness that brings it all together. The grapefruit tequila is incredibly easy to make, though you'll need to plan ahead.

Ingredients
1 ½ fluid ounces Grapefruit-infused Tequila (see page 19)
1 fluid ounce Grand Marnier
dry rosé, to top off
¼ fluid ounce grenadine
½ grapefruit slice and a cherry, to garnish

Instructions
Combine the tequila and Grand Marnier in a hurricane glass (or other tall glass) filled with ice. Top off with rosé. Slowly pour the grenadine around the inside of the glass. It will sink and gradually rise to mix with the other ingredients. Garnish with half a grapefruit slice and a cherry.

SWEET HONEY ROSÉ

(Makes 1)

There's a very simple cocktail called the bee's knees that
became a hit during Prohibition in America. It was used as
a way to doctor up the less-than-desirable "bathtub" gin of
the time by adding honey syrup and lemon juice. The Sweet
Honey Rosé reimagines this old-time favorite to create an
equally fascinating drink that mixes up in minutes. In this
recipe, gin is replaced with whiskey—a smooth blend like
Irish whiskey is a fantastic choice—and retains the honey
syrup and lemon juice. The final ingredient is, of course, rosé.
Almost any wine will do and it's best to experiment with a few
to find one that matches your taste. Some people may like
a sweeter rosé, such as a white zinfandel, while others may
prefer a wine with a drier profile.

Ingredients
½ fluid ounce honey
½ fluid ounce water
1 ½ fluid ounces whiskey
a splash of lemon juice
1 ½ fluid ounces rosé

Instructions
There are no secrets to making honey syrup: combine
equal parts honey and water and stir until you get a uniform
consistency. It's a simple trick that thins out the honey just
enough to make it easier to mix in cold drinks. Combine all
the ingredients in a cocktail shaker filled with ice. Shake well
and strain into a chilled cocktail glass.

LYCHEE GINGER MARTINI

(Makes 1)

A lychee tastes like a strawberry (hence the nickname "alligator strawberry") and it pairs wonderfully with many flavors, from citrus to cranberry, but it's also a surprising companion for ginger. It is becoming easier to find lychee-flavored liqueurs and syrups on the market, but the other option is to make one of these yourself, using fresh or canned fruits (which have had the inedible hulls removed). The ginger vodka can also be a homemade project because it's not the most common flavor among vodka brands. If you don't want to go to that extent, you can use unflavored vodka and enjoy a rosé lychee martini.

Ingredients
1 ½ fluid ounces lychee liqueur or syrup (see page 17 and below)
1 ½ fluid ounces Ginger-infused Vodka (see page 19)
1 ½ fluid ounces rosé
a lychee or lemon twist, to garnish

Instructions
Pour the ingredients into a cocktail shaker filled with ice and shake well. Strain into a chilled cocktail glass, then garnish with a lychee or lemon twist.

To make a lychee liqueur, add 4 fluid ounces of lychee syrup to 12 fluid ounces of vodka, adding more to taste, if desired.

SNOW ROSÉ

(Makes 1)

The Snow Rosé is one of the most beautiful drinks you'll have the pleasure of sipping. Whenever you shake a cocktail with pineapple juice, a luscious foam forms on top of the drink after straining. This cocktail takes full advantage of that because you'll drizzle pink rose water over the foam and swirl it gently to create the effect of rose petals on a bed of snow. Make sure your rose water is the food-safe variety, not a product made for cosmetic use. Some rose water is pink while others are clear. If you can only find the clear variety, stir in a small amount of rosé to give it a hint of color.

Ingredients
1 fluid ounce aged rum
1 fluid ounce rosé
1 fluid ounce pineapple juice
a splash of Simple Syrup (see page 15)
a drizzle of rose water

Instructions
Pour the rum, wine, juice, and syrup into a cocktail shaker filled with ice. Shake vigorously and strain into a chilled cocktail glass. Drizzle the rose water on top of the foam and give it a quick swirl with a spoon or a small stick.

Tip: If you have pesticide-free rose plants, you can harvest the petals to make your own rose water. Rinse the petals from two roses, then combine them in a small saucepan with 16 fluid ounces of distilled water and a teaspoon of vodka. Simmer, covered, for about 30 minutes, or until the petals become pale. Remove from the heat, strain, and bottle. This will keep in the refrigerator for 2 weeks (the vodka acts as a preservative).

WILD IRISH ROSÉ

(Makes 1)

Irish whiskey and rosé are a very nice duo and they find perfect harmony in the lovely Wild Irish Rosé, where they're sweetened with a combination of pomegranate and cherry liqueurs. Using a sparkling wine transforms this into an effervescent beverage that's fantastic anytime you feel the desire for a unique whiskey highball. Cherry Heering is called for specifically because it's one of the best cherry-flavored liqueurs available. It's sweet, with a deep red color, but it lacks that medicinal taste that is so common in spirits of this flavor, which is why it's a great choice for cocktails. The next best option is maraschino liqueur. It's a little drier, so it's a good option if you prefer drinks that are less sweet.

Ingredients

1 fluid ounce Irish whiskey
½ fluid ounce pomegranate liqueur
½ fluid ounce Cherry Heering
3 fluid ounces sparkling rosé, to top off
a dash of orange bitters
a cherry, to garnish

Instructions

Combine the whiskey and liqueurs in a collins glass filled with ice. Stir for 30 seconds, then top off with sparkling rosé. Add a dash of orange bitters and garnish with a cherry.

MIDNIGHT ROSÉ FLOAT

(Makes 1)

An ice cream float combines a soft drink with vanilla ice cream. Skip the soft drink and make yourself a delicious ice cream treat with rosé instead! The Midnight Rosé Float is a fun recipe that throws all pretentions associated with wine out of the window. It's definitely one of the most indulgent wine drinks you can mix up, but it also has a touch of class. For this recipe, you'll use a mix of brandy, Grand Marnier, and rosé as the liquid portion of the ice cream float. The hint of orange from the brandy-based liqueur adds a soft, sweet fruitiness that is intriguing against the other ingredients. You could even add another dimension by choosing an apricot or cherry brandy, if you like.

Ingredients
1 scoop vanilla ice cream
1½ fluid ounces brandy
¾ fluid ounce Grand Marnier
2 fluid ounces rosé
chocolate syrup and a raspberry, to garnish

Instructions
Place a scoop of ice cream in the bottom of a parfait glass and put it in the freezer while you mix the rest of the drink. In a cocktail shaker filled with ice, combine the brandy, Grand Marnier, and wine and shake well. Strain over the ice cream, then drizzle with chocolate syrup and garnish with a raspberry.

BOURBON

MATURED IN OAK CASKS

43% ALC/VOL

Vol. 700ml

ROSÉ COLLINS

(Makes 1)

The collins is a classic mixed-drink formula of a base spirit, combined with a sweetener, a sour element, and soda water. Any distilled spirit is up for grabs: whiskey and gin are the most popular, although vodka, rum, and tequila are also good choices. In the Rosé Collins, whiskey—specifically bourbon—is the spirit of choice, and the soda water is replaced with a sparkling rosé. The fun elements of this collins are the sweet and sour ingredients. It opts for honey syrup (a mix of equal parts honey and water) along with a muddle of cucumber slices and a lemon wedge. These add a fresh-produce spin on the drink that turns it into an absolute delight for the warmer seasons.

Ingredients

½ fluid ounce honey
½ fluid ounce water
3 cucumber slices
a lemon wedge
1½ fluid ounces bourbon
sparkling rosé, to top off
extra cucumber and lemon slices, to garnish

Instructions

Combine the honey and water and stir until you get a uniform consistency. In a highball glass, muddle the syrup, cucumber slices, and lemon wedge. Fill the glass with ice, add the whiskey, stir thoroughly, and top off with rosé. Garnish with a slice each of cucumber and lemon.

VIOLETS & ROSES

(Makes 1)

Crème de violette is an often overlooked liqueur, but it's a
perfect ingredient for rosé cocktails. This violet-flavored,
eye-catching purple liqueur offers a beautiful floral
fragrance and taste. It's the star of the aviation cocktail, a
delightful gin martini, and the Violets & Roses is a modern
adaptation of that classic, simply replacing the gin with rosé.
In keeping with its roots, you'll likely find it at its best when
made with a high-end Provençal rosé. The drier profile
mimics that of gin, and this cocktail really deserves the
best wine you feel comfortable pouring. When the violets
and wine are accented with the cherry of a dry maraschino
liqueur and fresh lemon juice, you will have an exquisite
cocktail that is guaranteed to impress anyone.

Ingredients
2 fluid ounces rosé
½ fluid ounce maraschino liqueur
¾ fluid ounce crème de violette
½ fluid ounce lemon juice
a lemon twist, to garnish

Instructions
Combine all of the ingredients in a cocktail shaker filled
with ice. Shake well and strain into a chilled cocktail glass,
garnishing with a lemon twist.

ROSEMARY & BASIL FIZZ

(Makes 1)

Finding drinks that you can make with ingredients from your own garden always makes the harvest that much more satisfying, and this one is the perfect drink to sit back with as you relax and survey the fruits of your labor. This is also a great recipe for anyone who enjoys homemade mixers. Sure, you may be able to find a cucumber vodka in the shops (and Hendrick's Gin is a good substitute), but it's a very easy infusion to make yourself if you plan ahead.

Ingredients
1½ fluid ounces Cucumber-infused Vodka (see page 19)
½ fluid ounce Rosemary–Basil Syrup (see page 17)
½ fluid ounce lime juice
3 fluid ounces sparkling rosé
a sprig of rosemary, to garnish

Instructions
Pour the ingredients in order into an ice-filled Mason jar (or another tall glass), finishing up with the wine. Stir well and garnish with a sprig of rosemary.

JASMINE TEA TINI

(Makes 1)

A tea-flavored martini is a great choice as an afternoon drink, and jasmine tea is a wonderful, fragrant option. It's particularly nice when paired with rosé in a simple and elegant vodka martini recipe. The Jasmine Tea Tini is easy to prepare and you can adjust each of the elements to suit your personal taste. Start by pouring equal parts of the vodka and rosé, then increase either while reducing the quantity of tea, if you like. Then add more of either the Simple Syrup or lemon juice as you see fit. This is also a lovely recipe to mix up by the jug and serve at a small gathering: keep everything in proportion and increase the pour of each ingredient according to the number of servings you need. You can stir it with ice in the jug, then pour it into cocktail glasses to serve.

Ingredients

1 fluid ounce vodka
1 fluid ounce rosé
2 fluid ounces jasmine tea, chilled
a splash of Simple Syrup (see page 15)
a splash of lemon juice
a jasmine flower or lemon twist, to garnish

Instructions

In a cocktail shaker filled with ice, combine the ingredients. Shake well and strain into a chilled cocktail glass. If available, garnish with a jasmine flower; otherwise use a long lemon twist.

TAYLOR'S

CINNAMON
SYRUP

SINCE 1988

Z

PINOT ROSÉ

POINSETTIA SANGRIA

(Makes 5)

Who says sangria should be reserved for summer? This wine punch is just as appropriate for winter celebrations as it is for any other time of year, especially if you have the right recipe. The Poinsettia Sangria plays up the best flavors of the Christmas season, and makes a wonderful addition to any holiday soirée. It features pomegranates and cranberries, both of which come into their prime as the weather begins to cool down, while the cinnamon syrup adds a warming touch that makes this drink a real winter delight.

Ingredients
2 pomegranates
2 fluid ounces Cinnamon Syrup (see page 17)
25 fluid ounces rosé
8 fluid ounces light rum
1 cup cranberries
2 oranges, sliced
extra cranberries or pomegranate arils (seeds), to garnish

Instructions
Remove the arils from the pomegranates and reserve a few for the garnish. Smash the rest of the arils in a bowl, then strain them so you are left with a fresh juice. Combine the juice with the remaining ingredients in a jug, stir well, and refrigerate overnight to allow the flavors to marry. Serve in tumblers or punch cups and garnish with cranberries or pomegranate arils.

PASSIONFRUIT SANGRIA

(Makes 12)

There's a lot going on in this very fruity sangria! It's a fun blend of tropical fruit flavors, including passionfruit, pineapple, and kiwi, so it's ideal for summer barbecues and pool parties. The recipe makes a lot of punch, too, so you can quench the thirst of all your guests with a single batch. As with any sangria, this one's all about the fresh fruit. Fresh lemon, orange, and kiwi are included, but if you spot passionfruit and pineapples at the grocery store, you can add some chunks of those as well. The Passionfruit Sangria is best with a sweeter rosé; white zinfandel is an excellent choice.

Ingredients
25 fluid ounces sweet rosé
8 fluid ounces brandy
16 fluid ounces passionfruit juice
16 fluid ounces pineapple juice
1 lemon, sliced
1 orange, sliced
2 kiwis, sliced
16 fluid ounces ginger ale

Instructions
Combine all of the ingredients except the ginger ale in a large bowl, stir well, and refrigerate overnight so the flavors blend and develop fully. When it's time to serve, add the ginger ale and ladle into punch cups. Kiwi slices make a great garnish, but they're not necessary if you ladle fruit into the glasses.

WHITE PEACH SANGRIA

(Makes 10)

Rosé is a perfect wine for a sangria featuring the sweet taste of white peaches. This punch is perfect for summer, when these delectable fruits make their annual appearance in shops everywhere. The recipe will provide enough for a small party, and all of your guests will enjoy this refreshing, light twist on the classic sangria. This sangria is not all about the peach, either! It also includes the tropical taste of a mango-flavored rum. Adding lemons and limes to the mix creates a bright, fruity drink that is unforgettable.

Ingredients
25 fluid ounces rosé
12 fluid ounces Mango-infused Rum (see page 19)
12 fluid ounces peach liqueur
4 white peaches, sliced
2 limes, sliced
2 lemons, sliced
20 fluid ounces soda water
extra peach slices, to garnish

Instructions
In a large jug or bowl, combine the wine, rum, liqueur, and all the sliced fruit. Refrigerate overnight to allow the flavors to marry. Before serving, add the soda water. Pour into glasses over ice (if you like) and garnish with slices of white peach.

GREEN GRAPE SANGRIA

(Makes 8)

Grapes make a fantastic sangria year-round and they're another fabulous pairing for rosé wine. In the Green Grape Sangria, the grapes actually serve as a substitute for ice, offering all of the chill with none of the dilution, and a little extra flavor. The base of this sangria is a still rosé, then a sparkling version is added at the end to give it a nice fizz. White grape juice is much lighter and less sweet than the regular purple juice, so it's a much better fit for this recipe. If you'd like, use freshly pressed green grape juice instead.

Ingredients
6 cups green grapes
2 lemons, sliced
25 fluid ounces still rosé
16 fluid ounces white grape juice
2 fluid ounces agave nectar
13 fluid ounces sparkling rosé

Instructions
Flash-freeze half of the grapes in a single layer in the freezer. Once frozen, they can be transferred to a bowl or bag for easy storage. In a glass, muddle the remaining grapes with the lemon slices, mashing them until all the juice is extracted. Strain out the lemon pieces and grape skins, leaving a clean juice behind. In a large jug, combine the grape–lemon juice with the still wine, white grape juice, and agave nectar. Stir thoroughly. Distribute the frozen grapes between 8 glasses, fill each three-quarters full with the sangria mix, then top with the sparkling rosé.

ORGANIC
VODKA
700ml   40%ALC

CARAMEL

SYRUP

CARAMEL APPLE SANGRIA

(Makes 10)

This punch provides a delicious way to celebrate fall. It uses the same caramel syrup you use to flavor your coffee, and by combining it with apple cider and freshly harvested apples, the sangria takes on a very seasonal flair. If you prefer, switch from plain vodka to a caramel-flavored vodka and use plain Simple Syrup (see page 15) to sweeten the punch instead. Since you'll likely make this in apple season, try to get your hands on some freshly pressed cider. And try to find the most flavorsome sparkling rosé you can. Although it plays a supporting role (bubbles) in this recipe, a lighter-profiled wine can easily get lost among all the other flavors.

Ingredients

8 fluid ounces vodka
2 fluid ounces caramel syrup
24 fluid ounces apple cider
3 red apples, cored and sliced
25 fluid ounces sparkling rosé
extra apple slices, to garnish

Instructions

In a jug, combine the vodka, syrup, and cider and stir. Add the apple slices and refrigerate overnight. Just before serving, add the sparkling wine. Serve in stemmed wine glasses (over ice if you prefer) and garnish with apple slices.

Tip: Apple slices will quickly turn brown due to oxidation, so to keep your garnish looking beautiful, dip your slices into a little lemon juice, then shake off the excess.

RASPBERRY LEMONADE SANGRIA
(Makes 8)

The peak of summer is an ideal time to mix up a Raspberry Lemonade Sangria. If you have a raspberry bush in the garden, it's even better and will make quick use of your harvest. Your guests will be delighted with the sweet, refreshing taste of this sangria, and you will be thrilled with how easy it is to make. The best advice is to keep it as fresh as possible—after all, summer is about enjoying the freshest ingredients—so take the time to make the lemonade and Simple Syrup from scratch. For the wine, any rosé will do, although this is the perfect recipe for a white zinfandel.

Ingredients
12 fluid ounces lemonade, bought or homemade (see below)
25 fluid ounces rosé
2 cups fresh raspberries
2 lemons, sliced
2 fluid ounces Simple Syrup (see page 15)
12 fluid ounces ginger ale
extra lemon slices and raspberries, to garnish

Instructions
To make fresh lemonade, stir together 1 part each of fresh lemon juice and Simple Syrup with 2 parts distilled water. Add more of any ingredient to suit your taste. Mix this lemonade together with the rosé, raspberries, lemon slices, and Simple Syrup in a large jug. Refrigerate overnight. Just before serving, add the ginger ale. Serve over ice, garnishing each glass with a slice of lemon and a few raspberries.

ROSÉ BERRY BLISS

(Makes 10)

When you serve the Rosé Berry Bliss at a party, it's bound
to brighten everyone's mood. This brilliant wine and
lemonade punch is unbelievably simple and has a tasty
fruit flavor that all your guests will love. And if you need
to make a larger batch, the quantities are easy to double
or triple. The beauty of this particular recipe is that the
ingredients are easy to find. While fresh blueberries are
preferable, frozen berries will do just fine out of season.
Most supermarkets now stock pink lemonade, and from
there, all you need is a bottle of rosé and some citrus-
flavored soda water.

Ingredients
25 fluid ounces rosé
1 cup blueberries
32 fluid ounces pink lemonade
34 fluid ounces lemon–lime soda water
extra blueberries, to garnish

Instructions
In a jug, combine the rosé, blueberries, and lemonade and stir
well. Set aside in the refrigerator for at least 1 hour to allow the
flavors to marry. Add the soda water just before serving.
Serve in flutes and garnish with blueberries.

ROSÉ ERDBEERBOWLE

(Makes 8)

Erdbeerbowle means "strawberry punch" in German and is a very popular summer party drink. This is possibly the most strawberry of all strawberry punches. It requires both still and sparkling wines, and making it is a bit of a process, so be sure to plan ahead. You'll need to macerate the strawberries in sugar and lemon juice for a couple of hours, then marinate them in the still rosé for a couple more. It is worth it, though, and your guests will appreciate your efforts!

Ingredients
6 cups strawberries, washed, hulled, and sliced
½ cup white granulated sugar
zest and juice of 2 lemons
25 fluid ounces still rosé
25 fluid ounces sparkling rosé
fresh mint leaves or lemon balm, to garnish

Instructions
Place the strawberries in a bowl and cover with the sugar. Add the lemon zest and juice to the strawberries, cover, and refrigerate for 2 hours. Separate the strawberries from the juice and set the juice aside. Pour the still rosé over the strawberries and marinate for 1 to 2 hours in the refrigerator. When ready to serve, transfer the strawberry–wine mixture to a punch bowl along with the strawberry juice, then add the sparkling wine. Ladle the punch into glasses, including plenty of strawberries in each. Garnish with mint or lemon balm and offer small forks or cocktail sticks so guests can skewer the berries as they drink.

CANTALOUPE PUNCH

(Makes 4)

When cantaloupe melons are in season, this easy punch is a
delightful addition to a small party. It's ideal for summer and
would be a nice complement to a casual brunch featuring
fresh fruits and delicate pastries. It's also a fun option at a
barbecue because it's such a good pairing for any grilled
meat or kebabs. The Cantaloupe Punch focuses on fresh
summer fruits, pairing the melon with sweet peaches.
There's even a little gin to give it a nice botanical twist; any
gin will do, even the lightly flavored and rosier ones. Since
the fruits are the only sweet elements in this recipe, you'll find
that it's best with a sweet rosé.

Ingredients
½ cantaloupe melon, peeled and cubed
2 peaches, sliced
4 fluid ounces gin
25 fluid ounces rosé

Instructions
Combine all the ingredients in a jug, stir well, then refrigerate
overnight to allow the flavors to marry. Serve in tall glasses,
making sure to include pieces of fruit in each.

ROSÉ BOWL

(Makes 4)

One of the most entertaining things you can do in a cocktail bar is to sit around a table with a group of friends slurping a boozy punch out of a fishbowl. It's a great time for all, and you can recreate that experience at home with the Rosé Bowl. This recipe features gin, and it's an excellent opportunity to use some of the lighter gins on the market— or any that take a unique approach to the juniper-forward standard. This punch is super-rosy and invigorating with its combination of rosé and grapefruit juice. Be sure to go all out on the fruits you mix into the ice! There are no rules, but the more fruit you add, the better and more exotic it will be.

Ingredients

4 fluid ounces gin
10 fluid ounces rosé
2 fluid ounces orange liqueur
8 fluid ounces ruby red grapefruit juice
grapefruit slices
seasonal berries

Instructions

Fill a fishbowl about halfway with ice and pour in all of the ingredients. Add the fruits, then stir well to mix everything together. Place the bowl in the middle of the table and use four long straws to enjoy it with your friends.

Tip: Fishbowl cocktail glasses are available to buy, and typically hold over 34 fluid ounces—more than enough for this recipe, including the ice and fruit. You can also use an actual fishbowl, but clean it very, very well if it's had previous inhabitants!